From
The
Heart

*Inspirational Messages
for readers in enjoying life*

Frederick W. Finn

authorHOUSE®

AuthorHouse™
1663 Liberty Drive
Bloomington, IN 47403
www.authorhouse.com
Phone: 1 (800) 839-8640

Published by AuthorHouse 06/17/2016

ISBN: 978-1-5246-0635-0 (sc)
ISBN: 978-1-5246-0634-3 (e)

Print information available on the last page.

*Any people depicted in stock imagery provided by Thinkstock are models,
and such images are being used for illustrative purposes only.
Certain stock imagery © Thinkstock.*

This book is printed on acid-free paper.

Contents

PSALM 37v 25

I have been young, and now is old, yet have I have not seen the Righteous forsaken nor his seed begging bread

To Neda E Finn
Wife Mother Best Friend

POEMS

The Company You Keep

You taught us if you run with wolves you will learn how to howl.
You taught us if you associate with eagles you would learn how to soar to great heights.
You taught us that a mirror reflects a man and woman true imagine of themselves.
You taught us that one important attribute in successful people is their impatience with negative thinking and negative acting people.
You taught us that your friends that won't stretch your dream would rather choke your dream.
You taught us that your friends that don't increase you would eventually decrease you.

You taught us that not everyone has the right to speak into your life.
You taught us that your friend that don't help you climb would want you to crawl.
You taught us that do not follow anyone who's not going anywhere in life.
You taught us with some people you spend an evening with others you invest it.
You taught us to be careful where you stop to inquire for directions along the road of life.
You taught us that every seed that you sow into fertile ground you could expect a harvest.

You taught us never receive counsel from unproductive people.
You taught us to never discuss our problems with someone incapable of contributing to the solution because those people who never succeed themselves are always first to tell you how. You taught us that growing older is evitable growing up is optional.
You taught us to watch "The Company You Keep" Amen

Inspired by Pastor Thomas W Riley Sunday's morning sermon to write my first poem February 10, 2001

The watchman opens the door this man, and the sheep listen To his voice and heed it; and he calls his own sheep by name and Brings (leads) them out. When he has brought his own sheep outside, he walks on before Them, and the sheep follow him because they know his voice. They will never (on any account) follow a strangers or recognize their call.
John 10:3-5 Amp

Follow The Leader

Follow the Leader that demonstrates values of integrity, morality and leadership ability.

Follow the Leader that will give you the guidance to overcome any obstacles in your life, because an obstacles is just an opportunity that is camouflage(Selah).

Follow the Leader by showing your obedience, consider your ways. The word says in all of your getting get understanding.

Follow the Leader not one who is not going anywhere, but one that will lead you in the direction to prosperity in all areas of your life.

Follow the Leader for their assignment, is to establish the word of GOD in the people for the life that GOD has promised for his people.

Follow the Leader's Guidance, Obedience and Direction (GOD) you must be diligent with applying those three principles for your life.

(GOD gives the anointing to those he appoint to lead) Follow The Leader

Also (JESUS) told them a parable to the effect that they always to pray
    and not to turn coward
(faint, lose heart and give up)
Luke 18:19 Amp

MEN MUST PRAY

Men Must Pray men must pray the word said men must pray

Men Must Pray have faith and belief in the words they say

Men Must Pray in the morning noon evening and every day

Men Must Pray establish their ground as the head and Lead the Way

Men Must Pray because all things are possible when GOD hear the
    words of men as they pray

Men Must Pray and let GOD direct every step that they take in their
    walk in faith

Men Must Pray because prayer builds spiritual strengthen in a special way

Men Must Pray men must pray along with fasting when they pray

The words in this poem is very simple to say but the message is so very
    vital to men because the words said Men Must Pray

BLESSED (Happy fortunate prosperous and enviable) is the man who walks and lives not in the counsel of the ungodly (following their advice, their plans and purpose) nor stands (submissive and Inactive) in the path where sinners walk, nor sits down (to relax and rest) where the scornful(and the mockers gather.

But his delight and desire are in the law of the Lord, and on His law (the precepts, the instructions, the teachings of GOD) he habitually meditates (ponder and studies) by day and by night.
Psalm 1:1-2 Amp

BLESSED

Blessed are the man woman and child that praises GOD with a smile

Blessed is being a blessings to all of GOD's children near and far

Blessed is knowing the ultimate sacrifice that JESUS had to pay

Blessed is having the will to choose life for JESUS paved the way

Blessed is consistently walking in faith allowing yourself no escape

Blessed is to overcome life daily challenges that may come your way

Blessed is giving GOD the FATHER the glory honor and praise always

Blessed is thanking our Heavenly FATHER for his Mercy and Grace

Blessed are all the readers of this poem today know that you are blessed when the morning comes and you lived to see another day. U-R-BLESSED

No one has greater love (no one has shown stronger affection) than to lay down (give up) his own life for his friend
John 15:13 Amp

FRIENDSHIP

A friend we often claim many but that is not always true

A friend is a person that shown honesty loyalty and truth

A friend will be with you despite whatever you go through

A friend lift your spirit up when you choose to let it down

A friend understand your life challenges upon your crown

A friend will not spread gossip conflict backbiting or strife

A friend in a true relationship invest only love for your life

A friend prays for you in the morning noon and every night

A friend yes we often claim many as we take our walk in life

A friend we have for sure when GOD choose the ones for our life

JUST A THOUGHT

LISTENING OBEYING LEARNING (LOL)

Listening is an act of hearing not only with your physical ear, but also with your spiritual ear. The act of Obeying must be your will lining up with God's instructions to overcome any challenges in your life. Learning is a life long process of skills for you to learn to live and ENJOY life.(LOL)

"Just a Thought"

LOVE & CARE

Love is God and God is love and his love is unconditional. Care is a human emotion to show concern that sometimes based on the circumstances or situations comes with conditions.

"Just a Thought"

LITTLE THINGS

Enjoy the little things in life first, because eventually throughout your life journey big things will come in there appointed time.

"Just a Thought"

LIVE and LEARN

Everyday that you live learn and as you learn live. Whatever you learn in your life can help you live; ENJOY life.

"Just a Thought"

A BELIEVER

Believer's belief system is only belief until the point of their execution. In other words if you don't execute in your belief system you are operating in unbelief.

"Just a Thought"

DELIVERANCE

When you accept JESUS CHRIST as your LORD and SAVIOR. Your Deliverance is a life long daily process. Not a One Time Event.

"Just a Thought"

HEARING & LISTENING

There is a definitive difference in Hearing and Listening. The process is simple you Hear words with your outer ear. Listening to the words are with your inner ear. The fact is Hearing and Listening to words will cause a change in your life.

"Just a Thought"

NOW

Now consider this, every time that you look at yourself in the mirror you are a individual winner in life. Your first challenge was your race to be birthed in your mother's womb. When you spell now backwards it spells Won.

"Just a Thought"

PRAYERS

A prayer can be audible or silent when you pray to our Heavenly Father. He knows all and hears all of our prayers. We can rest in assurance of his words. That all of his promises are yea and Amen!

"Just a Thought"

FIVE SENSES

One: Hearing consist of getting an understanding when you truly hear with your spiritual ear.

Two: Seeing goes beyond the two eyes we have to see through for sight.

Three: Smelling is like old memories of something good or bad.

Four: Taste reminds you of things bitter and sweet.

Five: Touching can be warm or cold.

In our everyday life we use these senses, for some people they face certain challenges but, through it all they overcome each one.

"Just a Thought"

DANGER or FEAR

Danger exist daily which is a reality of living. Fear is a "Spirit" the choice is yours to accept living with Fear in your life.

"Just a Thought"

SEVEN or TEN SECONDS

Time is so very precious down to the very seconds of life. So remember this when you need to make an attempt to reach out and call someone. If that person live in your area code it takes only Seven Seconds out of your area Ten Seconds.

"Just a Thought"

AWARD or REWARD

Man will give you an Award for what you have accomplished in your life. Our Father (GOD) in heaven will Reward you for your acts of obedience in your life.

"Just a Thought"

LIFECYCLE

Our cycle of life begins with defined numbers which includes a time, day, month and year. Our cycle of life ends with a year, month, day and time.

"Just a Thought"

AHA

Everyone in their life time will experience an AHA moments. Always Happening Again (AHA))

"Just a Thought"

BETTER

When you know better do better, but if you don't know better ask.

"Just a Thought"

YESTERDAY TOMORROW FUTURE

Yesterday is behind you, wake up to enter into your Tomorrow. As you close out Tomorrow get ready to walk into your Future.

"Just a Thought"

GIFTS

The greatest gifts that I ever had came from GOD, I called them Dad and Mom.

"Just a Thought"

LADDER

A ladder has steps for the purpose to place you on different levels of heights until you reach the top. When you look at your life, picture a ladder as you take those steps to new levels in your life to reach your goals.

"Just a Thought"

FUTURE

Often when we think about the future our thoughts reflect towards, day's, weeks, months, years and decades. The fact of the matter is the future is really our next Heart beat. The future is only a second away what about that.

"Just a Thought"

WINNER

The race that we won makes us winners in life, many entered the race but you were the winner. You crossed the finish line, a certain day, date and time. That race which I am referring to is your life that God gave you. That glorious race is your physical birth.

"Just a Thought"

OVERCOMING CONQUERING DELIVERENCE (OCD)

Overcoming any challenge that we might encounter in life. Our Faith, Confidence and Courage will allow us to become a Conqueror over that challenge. The Deliverance process, is a daily life long battle for us all.

"Just a Thought"

GETTING vs. GIVING (G2G)

Getting is an act of your will to receive something. Giving is an act of your will to release something.

"Just a Thought"

ANY-BODY or RIGHT-BODY

We should not be so quick to accept advice from Any-Body speaking words over our life.
Here is my point do a check up from the neck up to ensure that the Right-Body speaks over your life.

"Just a Thought"

FIGHTING OPPOSITION CONSTANTLY USING SCRIPTURES (FOCUS)

When you are faced with Spiritual Warfare, it vital for us to know and understand your opponent.
The fact of this matter is because the word of GOD says the battle is not YOURS it's the LORD!

"Just a Thought"

WHAT ARE YOU SAYING (WAYS)

Often time's people are quick to repeat this saying?. Do you know what I am sayings over and over again. The fact of the matter is this! I heard what you said but What Are You Saying check your (WAYS).

"Just a Thought"

U-N-I-T-Y (UNITY)

Unity is power to make changes in many areas in life. Here is my breakdown for that acronym for unity. If U are Not in IT then tell yourself Y?

"Just a Thought"

NEEDS vs. WANTS

The letter N is before the letter W, that is the order of the alphabet correct? As human beings we often place our wants before our needs which is totally out of order. If we begin to understand to focus on our needs in life, all of our wants will come in due season.

"Just a Thought"

HEALTH vs. WEALTH

Acknowledge this letter H comes way before the letter W in the alphabet. Let's define Health and Wealth ; Health: A condition of being sound in Body, Mind or Spirit. Wealth : Abundance of valuable materials possessions or resources. Health vs. Wealth what is your choice?

"Just a Thought"

CHANGE

We can change and choose the things to do in the course of our day. We can not change people because submission is the act of the heart. We must be willing to let God change us first, then pray for the people around us to change.

"Just a Thought"

INTELLIGENCE QUOTIENT vs. EMOTIONAL QUOTIENT

IQ vs. EQ is the process in which we as human beings go through daily. In other words the rational (IQ) verses the irrational (EQ). At the end of the day, IQ will always win over EQ because you must finish with a rational agreement.

"Just a Thought"

ATTITUDE

Your attitude is a choice be it positive or negative on how you view life. Positive Mental Attitude (PMA) determine your path to success. Negative Mental Attitude (NMA) determine your path not to succeed.

"Just a Thought"

SMILE

A smile is contagious place one on your face and see. It only takes seventeen facial muscles at work to make a smile. It takes thirty seven muscles at work to make a frown. What do you choose?

"Just a Thought"

OPTION

Living a long life and getting older is evitable growing up is your option.

"Just a Thought"

ENVIRONMENT

Do not adjust to the environment, but cause the environment your in to change around you.

"Just a Thought"

CONFIDENCE

We should never lose our confidence because it's our gift for victory !

"Just a Thought"

UPS & DOWNS

As human beings we all have our ups and downs in life. We can probably say we experience more downs than ups. Always remember this, we have a choice when it comes to the downs.

"Just a Thought"

MINDSET

A Mindset is you will listen to accept change. A Setmind you will only hear change. Which one do you choose?

"Just a Thought"

SHORT CUTS

When you take to many short cuts in life. The reality is you could be cutting things short for your life.

"Just a Thought"

PEACE

Having peace in your life is an inside job, you must first make the minor inside adjustment to have a healthy and prosperous soul.

"Just a Thought"

BENEFIT of DOUBT

If you say that you gave a person the benefit of doubt understanding the process. The letter B comes before the letter D in the alphabet. Therefore do not be so quick to DOUBT by passing judgment on a person.

"Just a Thought"

HAPPINESS

It is common for every human being to experience different levels of happiness in their life. Here are some I just want to share with you. Beginning with UNHAPPINESS, CHASING HAPPINESS, and CAUSING HAPPINESS The most important level of HAPPINESS, FINDING HAPPINESS with GOD!

"Just a Thought"

SEASONS

In our circle of life people are like the seasons. In other words people will come into your life for a period of time then leave.

"Just a Thought"

THE SEED

Always remember, whatever seed a human beings sows or plants into ground. The product of the harvest will be either positive or negative, because it all about the ground and the seed.

"Just aThought"

NEWS

Noticeable Evidence Will Surface (NEWS) that's a reality of life information given to us freely every day about facts going on in this world.

"Just a Thought"

BACKSLIDE

The word BACKSLIDE is misunderstood because here is the complete process. If a person BACKSLIDE they will eventually SLIDEBACK with our prayers.

"Just a Thought"

POWER

A definition for Power is having the ability to do something, with strength and force. If you dropped the letter P and R the word left is OWE. So understand that you OWE yourself to know the Power that you have living inside you. Genesis 2V26

"Just a Thought"

BETTER /HALF

GOD created man a whole man, then he created a whole woman from man which made them both complete beings. I often hear people say they must find their Better Half. So think about this if GOD is in the works of making things complete, what Better Half are people talking about they must find.

"Just a Thought"

BEAUTY

Having physical beauty it will fade over a period of time, but having class that last forever.

"Just a Thought"

WEAPONS

Isaiah 54 v17 New Living Translation (NLT) Bible reads; But in that coming day no weapon turned against you will succeed. You will silence every voice raised up to accuse you. The word YOU appears three times in that verse. Therefore it's all about you being successful over the weapons against You.

"Just a Thought"

EVIL &?

Evil is a spirit, some definitions are; very bad corrupt, immoral and wicked. Check this out! add the letter D in front of evil what does it spells?

"Just a Thought"

ANGER &?

The human emotion of anger must be controlled for this reason. Check this out! the next level of anger, add D in front of anger what does it spell?

"Just a Thought"

PRE/RE

PRE means before and Re means again. Consider this think positive before (PRE) you act, because you do not need to do the same negative things over again (RE).

"Just a Thought"

OUTSIDE & INSIDE

Outside is the external makeup (Flesh) of a man and woman which can be seen in a untrue state of that person. Inside is the interior makeup (Spirit) of a man and woman which is known by GOD.

"Just a Thought"

HEALTH vs. WEALTH

HEALTH is a condition of being sound in Body, Mind and Spirit. WEALTH is abundance of valuable materials possessions or resources. HEALTH vs. WEALTH what is your choice?

"Just a Thought"

MESS-UP

In everyone's life their will come a time when you will Mess-UP. The end results is when you Clean-UP what you Mess-UP.

"Just a Thought"

DOORS

It's important for you to know about the opening of doors in your life. Consider knocking and asking GOD, he can open doors for you in your season that man can not close.

"Just a Thought

U-TURNS

GOD allows U-TURNS for his children to get back on the right path without giving them a ticket.

"Just a Thought"

SILENCE

There is a time to keep silence, and a time to speak; Always remember this Silence can never be misquoted.

"Just a Thought

THE LOOK

You should not look down at a person's situation. The twist is you never know you might have to look up to that same person.

"Just a Thought"

PRAISE & ACCOLADES

All the Glory, Worship, Honor and Praise shall be given to GOD. To men and women give them the accolades.

"Just a Thought"

SUNLIGHT & LIGHT

Sunlight exposure is essential for emotional and physical health, but exposure to the Light of JESUS is essential for spiritual health.

"Just a Thought"

USE IT

An old clique says if you don't use it you will lose it. Here is the fact about that saying, if you don't use it you will be judged.

"Just a Thought"

BALANCE

The importance to having balance in your life is to be level with your understanding of matters in making the right decisions.

"Just a Thought"

TRUTH & LIE

The truth comes from the Spirit of man or woman because the spirit is truth. A lie comes from a man or woman living with an unhealthy soul.

"Just a Thought

CHOSEN & PICKED

From the beginning of time GOD has chosen people to do his will here on earth. Also from the beginning of time Man has hand picked people to do his works here on earth (Selah)

"Just A Thought"

PREACHER

A person either male of female who talks to people about living life according to the words of the Bible. If you drop the P and ER in Preacher the word become Reach. Keeping that in mind, Reach is a verb; one definition: to get in place.

"Just a Thought"

CHOICES

It will come a time when every human being will make choices in their lives here are few;

Love / Hate Happy / Sad, Peace / War, Succeed / Fail and Right / Wrong.

"Just a Thought"

EXPOSURE

Exposure can be positive or negative depending on what you have been exposed to in your life.

"Just a Thought"

ENTERTAIN

The kingdom of Heaven entertain the Spirit of man. The worldly ways of earth entertain the flesh of man.

"Just a Thought"

BIG

The word BIG does not spell Bad remember the bible story of David and Goliath.
BIG means; Believe In GOD. Selah

"Just a Thought"

LIVE

We must live to change because when you are living and remain the same are you really living

"Just a Thought"

TEST

If you do not pass the test you can not share your testimony

"Just a Thought"

THE WORD

The word of GOD changes lives you must first believe and receive the promises.

"Just a Thought"

WAITING

Waiting is the process of time which is out of our control. In other words just keep waiting your time will come.

"Just a Thought"

EVERYDAY

Everyday is a good day when you wake up, because yesterday was your past and you will never see that day again.

"Just a Thought"

THINK ABOUT IT?

JOURNEYS

Having feet and the ability to walk you can cross over many lands
Having an automobile you can travel down many roads across this
    country

Having a ship you could sail the oceans and the seven seas
Having an airplane you can fly high in the sky
Having uses of those things above your journeys will take time

The thought process travel at the rate of 24 billion feet per second that's
    a fact
So when you think of a journeys in your life whether Past or Present it
    takes no time
The past is yesterday and the present is today renew your mind for your
    future because
that is the journey that will come one day.

Think about IT?

LEADERSHIP

If we meditate on this word Leadership it carries awesome power(check
    this out)
If you use the first four leters it spells Lead add two more letters it spells
    Leader
If you add the last four letters you get Leadership. Everybody deserve
    outstanding
Leadership.

If we define Lead it means; a position at the front, guide or direct on a
    course of direction
If we define Leader it means; a person who has command authority or
    influence, a member presiding over the whole body, capacity to lead

If we define Ship it means; a vessel, the body of persons participating ina specified activity having membership.

If you sum everything all up LEADERSHIP is simply this one person appointed. To Lead as the Leader of the Ship; direct command and specify instructions to a body of people.

Think about IT?

PLACES THINGS & PEOPLE

When you hink about the acronym PTP meaning Places Things and People.
We have the ability to only change two out of the three in our daily life(check this out)
We can change and choose the places where we decide to travel

We can change and choose the things to do in the course of our day
We can not change people because; submission is the act of the heart
We must ask GOD to help us change first; then change the people around us.

Think about IT?

THE LINE-UP

Have you ever gave thought of how important it is to Line-UP? (check this out)
A line-up begins in the womb of a mother for the baby to enter into this world
A line-up is when a baby positions his or her self feet when taking those first steps
A line-up for a professional race determine the starting point to count down

A line-up helps the law sometimes to identify a person who committed a crime

A line-up is part of our daily life challenges everyday that we live here
on earth

A line-up you see is very vital; you read the message above! Now
LINE-UP when you Hear, Know and Understand the true words
of GOD and stay on his LINE-UP.

Think about IT?

PULPIT

When you hear the word Pulpit our first thoughts on this word; we
think church

That word Pulpit is very powerful when you meditate about it (check
this out)

From the Pulpit the Leader of the church speaks to the congregation
about GOD's word

The word Pulpit if separated becomes a verb and noun; the breakdown
is pull and pit

The word pull defined means; tugging, drawing, dragging and
stretching words of action

The word pit defined means; futility, misery, below and hell words of
a place and things

The close to this message is simple; the next time your hear words from
the pulpit

Submit to the Leaders "Guidance Obedience & Direction" to be pulled
from the pits in our lives.

Focus above GOD selah.

Think about IT?

QUOTES

MIRACLES

You were made for miracles and miracles are for you.

Apostle Leroy Thompson Sr.

THANKSGIVING

Thanksgiving attract GOD into your life because he reflect on your appreciation of giving thanks

Bishop Daniel Robertson Jr.

OK

It's not OK just being OK

Bishop Daniel Robertson Jr.

WRONG

There's nothing wrong in being wrong, but there's something wrong in staying wrong once you have been corrected.

Pastor Phillip Gaillard

CAREER & CALLING

A Career is what you are paid for. A Calling is what you was made for.

Broderick Steven "Steve" Harvey

LEARN

Everyday that you live Learn and as you Learn live Enjoy Life

Frederick W Finn

FEAR

Fear is a "SPIRIT" a human being fear can be their unwillingness to learn.

Neda E Finn

PASS vs. FUTURE

The Pass is memory lane and the Future is a mystery right now.

Simone'

Granddaughter Age 10

MARRIAGE

Marriage is like a 360 degrees turn it's beautiful when two are together as one cirlce

Simone'
Granddaughter Age 11

Acronyms/Holynyms

BIBLE

Believers Instructions Before Leaving Earth

ISSUES

I See Serious Unresolved Essential Situation

BUSY

Being Under Satan Yoke

PUSH

Pray Until Something Happen

FEAR

False Evidence Appearing Real

ASAP

Always Say A Prayer

PRESS

Positioning Reaching Exercising Saving Souls

ASK

Always Seek Knowledge

YOKED

Your Obedience Knowledge Eliminates Distractions

BAD

Blessed And Delivered

AWOL

Always Worship Our Lord

YOLO

You Only Live Once

GOSSIP

Given Opportunity Spreading Someone Information Publicly

LUST

Living Under Satan Traps

SOS

Save One Soul

THUG

True Hero Under God

LACK

Listen Analyze Communicate Know

KEYS

Knowing Elevates Your Spirit

GPS

GOD Positioning Souls

LOL

Listen Obey Learn

BIG

Believe In GOD

WOW

Worship Overcomes Warfare

ADN

Any Day Now

GROW

GOD Rewards Obedient Worshippers

DIY

Do It Yourself

THE BIBLE ABC's

A=AWESOME

B=BELIEVER

C=CONFIDENCE

D=DELIEVERED

E=ELEVATE

F=FAITH

G=GRACE

H=HOLY

I=INTERNAL

J=JOY

K=KINGDOM

L=LOVE

M=MAGNIFICENT

N=NOBLE

O=OBEDIENCE

P=PRAISE

Q=QUENCH

R=RESURRECTION

S=SAVIOR

T=TEMPERANCE

U=UNITY

V=VICTORY

W=WORSHIP

X=X-RAY (INSIDE JOB)

Y=YIELD

Z=ZOE

Favorite Scriptures

PLASMS 23 New King James Version {KJV}

The Lord the Shepherd of His People

THE LORD is my shepard; I shall not want. He maketh me to lie down in green pasttures; he leadeth me beside the still waters. He restoreth my soul; he leadeth in the paths of righteousness for his name's sake. Yea, thought I walk through the valley of the shadow of death, I will fear no evil; for thou art with me; thy rod and thy staff they comfort me. Thou prepares a table before me in the presence of mine enemies; thou anointest my head with oil; my cup runneth over. Surely goodness and mercy shall follow me all the days of my life; and I will dwell in the house of the LORD for ever.

PROVERBS 3v5-6 New King James Version {KJV}

Guidance for the Young

Trust in the LORD with all thine heart; and lean not unto thine own understanding. In all thy ways acknowledge him, and he shall direct thy paths

NUMBERS 23v19 New King James Version (KJV)

Balaam's Second Prophecy

"God is not a man, that He should lie, Nor a son of man, that He should repent. Has He said, and will He not do? Or has He spoken, and will He not make it good?

DEUTERONOMY 28 1-2 New King James Version (NKJV)

Blessings on Obedience

Now it shall come to pass, if you diligently obey the voice of the Lord your God, to observe carefully all His commandments which I command you today, that the Lord your God will set you high above all nations of the earth. And all these blessings shall come upon you and overtake you, because you obey the voice of the Lord your God

MALACHI 3V8 New King James Version {KJV}

Do Not Rob God

"Will a man rob God? Yet you have robbed Me! But you say, In what way have we robbed You?' In tithes and offerings.

MATTHEWS 6v7-13 The Message (MSG)

Pray with Simplicity

"The world is full of so-called prayer warriors who are prayer-ignorant. They're full of formulas and programs and advice, peddling techniques for getting what you want from God. Don't fall for that nonsense. This is your

Father you are dealing with, and he knows better than you what you need. With a God like this loving you, you can pray very simply. Like this: Our Father in heaven, Reveal who you are. Set the world right; Do what's best— as above, so below. Keep us alive with three square meals. Keep us forgiven with you and forgiving others. Keep us safe from ourselves and the Devil. You're in charge! You can do anything you want! You're ablaze in beauty! Yes. Yes. Yes.

MATTHEWS 6v33 New Living Translation (NLT)

Teaching about Money and Possessions

Seek the Kingdom of God above all else, and live righteously, and he will give you everything you need.

LUKE 6v38 New King James Version {KJV}

Do Not Judge

Give, and it will be given to you: good measure, pressed down, shaken together, and running over will be put into your bosom. For with the same measure that you use, it will be measured back to you."

JOHN 3v16 New King James Version (KJV)

True Love

For God so loved the world, that he gave his only begotten Son, that whosoever believeth in him should not perish, but have everlasting life

JOHN 10 v10 New King James Version {KJV}

Jesus the Good Shepherd

The thief does not come except to steal, and to kill, and to destroy. I have come that they may have life, and that they may have it more abundantly.

GALATIANS 5v 22-26 New King James Version (KJV)

Walking in the Spirit

But the fruit of the Spirit is love, joy, peace, longsuffering, kindness, goodness, faithfulness, gentleness, self-control. Against such there is no law. And those who are Christ's have crucified the flesh with its passions and desires. If we live in the Spirit, let us also walk in the Spirit. Let us not become conceited, provoking one another, envying one another.

PHILIPPIANS 4 v 8-9 New King James Version {KJV}

Meditate on These Things

Finally, brethren, whatever things are true, whatever things are noble, whatever things are just, whatever things are pure, whatever things are lovely, whatever things are of good report, if there is any virtue and if there is anything praiseworthy—meditate on these things. The things which you learned and received and heard and saw in me, these do, and the God of peace will be with you

PHILIPPIANS 4 v13 New King James Version {KJV}

Generosity

I can do all things through Christ who strengthens me.

COLOSSIANS 3v 23-24 New King James Version {KJV}

The Christian Home

And whatever you do, do it heartily, as to the Lord and not to men, knowing that from the Lord you will receive the reward of the inheritance; for you serve the Lord Christ.

REVELATION 4v11 New King James Version {KJV}

The Throne Room of Heaven

You are worthy, O Lord, To receive glory and honor and power; For You created all things, And by Your will they exist and were created."

Printed in the United States
By Bookmasters